THE BLITZ

Liz Gogerly

Illustrated by Adam Hook

HODDER
Wayland

an imprint of Hodder Children's Books

Text copyright © 2002 Hodder Wayland
Illustrations copyright © 2002 Adam Hook

Project manager: Louisa Sladen
Designer: Peta Morey

Published in 2002 by Hodder Wayland
an imprint of Hodder Children's Books

British Library Cataloguing in Publication Data
Gogerly, Liz
The Blitz. - (Beginning History)
1. World War, 1939-45 - Campaigns - Great Britain - Juvenile literature
2. World War, 1939-1945 - Aerial operations, German - Juvenile literature
3. Great Britain - History - Bombardment, 1944-1945 - Juvenile literature
I. Title
941'.084

ISBN 0 7502 3790 2

Printed and bound in Italy

Hodder Children's Books
A division of Hodder Headline Limited
338 Euston Road, London NW1 3BH

Picture Acknowledgements
The publishers would like to thank the following for allowing their pictures to be
reproduced in this publication: The Imperial War Museum *back cover, title page,* 3,
5, 6 (top and bottom), 7, 8 (top and bottom), 15 (bottom), 18; Peter Newark
Picture Library 4, 9, 10, 15 (top), 21 (top); Topham Picturepoint 12, 14, 16, 20;
Popperfoto/Fox Photos 13; Popperfoto 21 (bottom).

While every effort has been made to secure permission, in some cases it has
proved impossible to trace copyright holders.

Contents

It's War!   **4**

When the Siren Sounds   **6**

Preparing for the Worst   **8**

The Blitz Hits London   **10**

The British Spirit   **12**

Pulling Together   **14**

'Business as Usual'   **16**

Bombs Blast Britain   **18**

'We Shall Never Surrender'   **20**

Glossary   **22**

Further Information   **23**

Index   **24**

It's War!

On 3 September 1939, people across Britain waited for the Prime Minister, Neville Chamberlain, to speak on the radio. They wanted to know if there was going to be a war against Germany. The German leader, Adolf Hitler, wanted to make Germany the strongest country in the world, ruling over other countries. By early 1939, German soldiers had already invaded Austria and Czechoslovakia. Then, on 1 September 1939, the Germans invaded Poland. Britain and France warned Hitler that they would help Poland if the Germans didn't leave. Hitler didn't listen.

Adolf Hitler watches as German soldiers march into Poland. In the next year, Germany invaded Denmark, Norway, France, Belgium, Luxembourg and the Netherlands.

'War declared!' – now everyone in Britain had to pull together to win the war.

A family listens to the Prime Minister on the radio. Just half an hour later, the first air-raid sirens were heard in London. But it was a false alarm.

▼

When Chamberlain started to speak, British people were nervous. It was a terrible shock when they were told: 'This country is at war with Germany.'

When the Siren Sounds

Children, as well as adults, were given gas masks. Here, at school, everyone has to practise using their gas masks – including the teacher! ▶

This war would be different to the First World War of 1914–1918. People expected Hitler to bomb British cities. Ordinary people, not just soldiers, would be killed. Everyone got ready in case Hitler attacked. First, there was the blackout. At night, any light that might be seen by German planes had to be put out or hidden. Gas masks were also given to everyone because the Germans might drop bombs containing poisonous gas.

LOOK OUT IN THE BLACK-OUT

▲ During the blackout, people had to cover all the lights on their cars. There were no street lights either, so there were lots of road accidents.

Public air-raid shelters were built in towns. Families were given Anderson shelters for their gardens. Some people made shelters under their stairs. And everyone practised the air-raid drill. When the Air-Raid Precautions (ARP) wardens sounded a siren there was a rush to the shelters. The siren made a wailing sound. One day soon that sound would mean that German planes were ready to drop their bombs on Britain.

Anderson shelters were built for six people. How many people can you see in this picture – do you think it's comfortable?

Preparing for the Worst

In September 1939, nearly three million children were evacuated from Britain's towns and cities. They were taken by railway to be looked after by people who lived in villages and towns in the countryside. Bombs might fall on factories, gasworks, railways and ports, but the children would be safe.

to hear that you and the baby are now away, safe in the country. It's grand too, to know that you are both so happy and comfortable the... Will you pleas... thank Mrs R...

Thank you SAYS THE SOLDIER

CARING FOR EVACUEES IS A NATIONAL SERVICE

ISSUED BY THE MINISTRY OF HEALTH

▲ Mothers with young children were also evacuated. The government made posters to thank the people who looked after them.

◄ These young children are about to leave London for the countryside. How do you think they feel about it?

For months no German bombs fell.
People started to call it the 'Phoney
War'. Then, in August 1940, German
bombs accidentally fell on London.
In return, the new British Prime Minister,
Winston Churchill, ordered the
bombing of Germany's capital city,
Berlin. Hitler was furious. So Britain
was prepared for the worst.

▲ The first fighting took place in the air. In July 1940, the Battle of Britain started in the skies above the south of England. The British had a new weapon – a little plane called the Spitfire.

The Blitz Hits London

The word 'blitz' comes from the German word 'blitzkrieg', which means 'lightning war'. Hitler planned air raids by German bomber planes on major British cities to be as quick and frightening as a lightning strike. He wanted to scare the British into surrendering.

Late in the afternoon of 7 September 1940, nearly one thousand German planes crossed the English Channel. They approached the main industrial areas in London's docklands and the East End. People below heard the roar of the planes' engines. The warning sirens began to wail. Some people ran to the shelters, but the bombs were already falling. The Blitz had begun. The Germans bombed factories, warehouses and the gasworks, but they also hit houses. Other parts of the city were bombed too. By dawn, 430 Londoners had been killed and 1,600 were badly hurt.

▲ On that day in September 1940, there were lots of planes in the sky. From a distance, some people thought they looked like birds.

Lots of bombs ▶ fell on London, hitting people's homes, and making large holes in the streets. Can you guess what has happened to this bus?

10

88 ACTON GREEN

GT 5058

SWAN VESTA

The British Spirit

The next day, Churchill visited bombed areas. People had lost their homes, families and friends but they were delighted to see him. 'It was good of you to come Winnie,' they shouted. 'We can take it. Give it them back!' They didn't know that London would be bombed nearly every night for the next eleven weeks!

▲ Winston Churchill gives his famous 'V for Victory' sign. He was certain that Britain would win the war.

◀ People tried to stay strong and cheerful during the Blitz, even when they had lost their homes, families and friends.

On 9 September, King George VI visited the East End. He talked with the homeless and listened to their sad stories. A few days later, Buckingham Palace was bombed during the night air raid. King George VI and Queen Elizabeth (now the Queen Mother) decided to stay in London. Like everybody else they wanted to show Hitler that their spirit could not be broken.

George VI and Queen Elizabeth look at the damage at Buckingham Palace. Queen Elizabeth said, 'I'm glad we've been bombed. It makes me feel I can look the East End in the face.'
▼

Pulling Together

Everyone pulled together during the long days and nights of the Blitz. Rescue work could be very dangerous. Firemen fought blazes, but more bombs sometimes fell into the very fires they were putting out. Doctors and nurses went into buildings that had been damaged by bombs and were in danger of falling down, to try and save the people trapped inside.

In this photograph, workers rescue a woman who has been trapped under this bombed building for 12 hours. The walls of the house look set to fall down at any moment.

 Danger! Unexploded Bomb – a London policeman bravely guards a bomb-site. At any moment, the bomb might go off!

A nice cup of tea! The Women's Voluntary Service took food and drink to rescue workers and homeless people.
▼

Other jobs were very difficult too. Ambulance drivers drove through streets destroyed by bombs. The ARP wardens often had to work in total darkness because of the blackout. It was their job to make sure that people were in the air-raid shelters when the sirens sounded. Many people did these jobs for no pay. They were proud to help win the war.

'Business as Usual'

'Victory, victory at all costs,' said Churchill in one of his speeches. Everyone looked forward to hearing Churchill on the radio. The Prime Minister made them feel that Britain could win the war. He also made them realize that they could keep going even if life was hard.

▲ After a street had been bombed, it was difficult to know where to deliver letters. This postman is trying to make sure he gives the post to the right person.

People spent most evenings in air-raid shelters. Shelters were uncomfortable and it was difficult to sleep. But people sang songs to cheer themselves up. Shops stayed open even when damaged by bombs. Postmen stumbled through streets full of rubble to deliver the mail. When the railways were hit, people walked miles to work. Signs saying 'Business as Usual' popped up everywhere. The British would not give in.

During the Blitz, Londoners used to sleep in the Underground. It was a very deep, safe air-raid shelter, away from the bombs.

▼

Bombs Blast Britain

The Second World War would hit ordinary people in Germany too. When British bombs were dropped on German cities, the Germans carried out more air raids. In November 1940, they bombed cities such as Liverpool and Birmingham. They targeted factories, but their bombs also killed thousands of people. When the town of Coventry was bombed in November 1940, the magnificent old cathedral was nearly ruined.

When Coventry Cathedral got bombed, it made British people more determined than ever to win the war.

▼

Hitler was amazed that he couldn't make the British surrender. In June 1941, he changed his plans and the air raids slowed down. But when Britain bombed historical German towns in early 1942, Hitler hit back. This time, bombs were dropped on beautiful old British towns such as York and Bath.

▲ The top picture shows the High Street in an old British town before any bombs have hit it.

The bottom picture shows the same High Street after it has been bombed. Now it is hard to recognize it as the same street.

'We Shall Never Surrender'

Churchill told the country, 'We shall fight on the beaches, we shall fight in the fields and in the streets, we shall never surrender.' Encouraged by his words, everybody in Britain played a part in the war against Germany. But, by June 1941, Britain needed help. Churchill turned to the USA. American soldiers joined the war in December 1941.

Keep the flag flying! ▶
Even after their homes were bombed, the British wouldn't give in.

From June to September in 1944, Germany attacked Britain with bombs once more. V-1 and V-2 rockets were the most frightening bombs ever made. They killed over 6,000 people in London. But, by now, American and British troops had invaded Europe. The Germans had retreated. Germany was losing the war. When Hitler killed himself in April 1945, Germany surrendered. After six long years the war had ended. The price had been high, but Britain had never surrendered!

The V-1 rocket was also called the 'buzz bomb' or 'doodlebug'. It was called Hitler's 'miracle weapon' because it didn't need a pilot.

▼

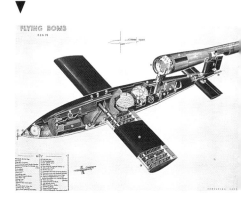

FLYING BOMB

Londoners took to the streets for a huge party on the day the war ended. At last, the war was over!

▼

Glossary

Air raid An attack by aeroplanes dropping bombs.

Air-raid drill A practice for when there is an air raid. This would mean putting on gas masks and running to the nearest air-raid shelter.

Air-Raid Precautions (ARP) warden Someone whose job it is to make sure that people are safe during an air raid. They would lead people to the air-raid shelters.

Anderson shelter A special kind of shelter made from iron. They were dug into the garden and covered with soil. A family of six could just about fit inside during an air raid.

Encouraged Given support and confidence to do something.

Evacuated When people have been moved away from somewhere because it might be dangerous.

Evacuees People who have been evacuated.

Historical Used to describe a person, place or thing that is old or is important in history.

Industrial To do with factories or businesses.

Invaded To have sent an army into another country and taken over their land.

Phoney Something which is false, or fake.

Rubble Broken bricks and stone from damaged buildings.

Siren A machine which makes a loud sound to warn people of an air raid.

Stumbled Walked with difficulty – often almost falling over.

Surrendering Giving up or agreeing that the enemy has won.

Wailing A long, sad sound – often used to describe people when they cry.

Further Information

Books to Read

World War II Evacuee (in the A Day in the Life of series) by Alan Childs (Hodder Wayland, 1999)

The Blitzed Brits (in the Horrible Histories series) by Terry Deary (Scholastic, 1996)

The Blitz (in the Britain in World War Two series) by Patricia Kendell (Hodder Wayland, 1996)

Air Raids (in the The History Detective Investigates Britain at War series) by Martin Parsons (Hodder Wayland, 1999)

The Home Front (in the The Past in Pictures series) by Fiona Reynoldson (Hodder Wayland, 1999)

Home in the Blitz by Marilyn Tolhurst (A & C Black, 1996)

Johnnie's Blitz by Bernard Ashley (Viking, 1995)

Websites You Can Visit

You can read stories from people who actually lived through the Blitz and find out how people sheltered themselves from the bombs.
www.bbc.co.uk/history/war/ wwtwo/homefront/blitz/blitz_ 3.shtml

You can visit the Imperial War Museum's website and find out what exhibitions are on there.
www.iwm.org.uk/lambeth/ index.htm

Places to Visit

The Cabinet War Rooms, Whitehall, London W1
(Telephone: 0891 600 140) – you can see Winston Churchill's secret underground offices where he planned the war.

The Imperial War Museum, Lambeth Road, London SE1
(Telephone: 020 7416 5000) – you can visit the Blitz Experience at this famous museum which covers the First and Second World Wars. See what an Anderson shelter really looked like and hear what it was like to have a bomb drop in the next street.

Index

Air-Raid Precautions (ARP)
    wardens 7, 15
air raids 10, 13, 18, 19
air-raid shelters 7, 15, 17
Anderson shelters **7**

Battle of Britain **9**
blackout **6**, 15
bombs 6, 7, 8, 9, 10, 14,
    15, 17, 18, 19, **21**
Buckingham Palace **13**

Chamberlain, Neville 4, 5
Churchill, Winston 9, **12**,
    16, 20
Coventry Cathedral **18**

East End 10, **11**, 13
evacuation **8**

First World War 6

gas masks **6**

Hitler, Adolf **4**, 6, 9, 10,
    13, 19, 21

King George VI **13**

'Phoney War' 9
Poland 4

Queen Elizabeth **13**

rescue workers **14**, **15**

siren 6, 7, 10, 15
Spitfire **9**
USA 20

V-1 rocket **21**
V-2 rocket 21